# 101 Simple Ways to

# Minister to Others

## STEPHANIE A. MAYBERRY

# 101 SIMPLE WAYS TO MINISTER TO OTHERS

## STEPHANIE A. MAYBERRY

All scriptures used in this text are taken from the
New American Standard Bible and the Amplified Bible.

First eBook Edition: October2011

ISBN-13: 978-1467936156
ISBN-10: 1467936154

Printed in the U.S.A.

# BOOKS BY STEPHANIE A. MAYBERRY

My Testimony

101 Simple ways to Minister to Others

7 Steps to a Godly Marriage

## HEALING FOR THE BATTERED SPIRIT SERIES

My Story is not Unique (a story about domestic violence)

Why I Stayed: Ministering to the Battered Spirit

More Valuable than Sparrows: Healing for the Battered Spirit

Ministering to the Battered Spirit: A Ministry Kit for Battling the Spirit of Abuse

## THE CHRISTIAN ASPIE SERIES

Fringe: My Life as a Spirit-Filled Christian with Asperger's Syndrome

More Fringe: My Growth as a Spirit-Filled Christian with Asperger's Syndrome

Deeper Fringe: My Joy as a Spirit-Filled Christian with Asperger's Syndrome (coming soon!)

The Christian Aspie: Notes from the Blog

## DEDICATION

When God first placed on my heart the burden to write, I had no
idea what it would involve. It was my husband who first told me
my writing was my ministry. It has been my husband who has
stood by me, supported me and encouraged me even when I felt
like quitting.

However, it has also been those dear readers who have written
me letters, sent me emails and connected with me on FaceBook
who have also encouraged me so very much.

So, I dedicate this book to all of those who have allowed God to
work through them to encourage me, push me and remind me
that I am doing His work and quitting is not an option.

I thank you all.

.

Dear Reader,

If the words in my books speak to you, resonate with you, touch you, please know it isn't really me, it is God speaking to you.

See, I am just a vessel that He uses to convey His message to you, to others. I am no great writer; I am just the obedient hand that holds the pen for the greatest author of all – my God.

He alone deserves all of the praise, all the glory.

Thank you so much for your support and encouragement. Each and every email, every word, every letter is such a treasure to me! I pray for your continued growth in your relationship with God. Forever walk in His Word and you will know blessings beyond your imagination.

God is so good, isn't He?

Stephanie Mayberry

*This is a book about ministering to others.*
*This is a book about "planting seeds."*

# CONTENTS

*"And Jesus came and spoke to them, saying, 'All authority has been given to Me in heaven and on earth. Go therefore and make disciples of all the nations, baptizing them in the name of the Father and of the Son and of the Holy Spirit, teaching them to observe all things that I have command you; and lo, I am with you always even to the end of the age."* ~Matthew 28:18-20

# 1

# INTRODUCTION

Jesus wants us to minister to others, to lead others to Him. However, many people hear "ministry" or "minister" and automatically think "preach." While preaching is a part of ministering to people, there are other ways to minister to them as well. This book gives you 101 ways that are simple yet effective. It is all about showing them the face of Jesus because you may be the only Bible they hear and the only Jesus they see.

The ideas in this book are quite diverse because people are diverse. What is comfortable for one person may not be comfortable for another. What reaches one person, may not reach another. It is important to be flexible when we minister to people because people aren't all the same with the same experiences, the same emotions, the same understanding, the same level of spirituality. In our enthusiasm, and if we are inflexible in our approach, we can run the risk of pushing people away, of missing crucial opportunities to open windows and illuminate dark corners.

In 1 Corinthians 10:31, Paul gives us some direction for ministering to others. "Therefore, whether you eat or drink, or whatever you do, do all to the glory of God" (1 Corinthians 10:31). So if everything you do should be done to the glory of God, then you can minister to others without preaching or teaching a Sunday school class. In fact, Paul goes on to say in verse 32, "Just as I also please all men in all things, not seeking my own profit, but the profit of many, that they may be saved."

See, Jesus wants us to meet people where they are in the way that they need to be ministered to or served. There are those who believe that they need to be forceful and "close the deal" when ministering to people – often by using fear. They believe that if they don't win that soul, they are failures before God. But that isn't the case. In fact, approaching ministry with that mission is likely to lead to feeling of discouragement and even a sense of failure because it just won't happen at times. Just because we are excited about the Word doesn't mean that others will receive it. And using this approach, with that goal in mind can be counterproductive to our efforts to lead others to Jesus.

Sometimes we are intended to set up the deal and someone else will come along and close it. We plant the seed and someone else waters it.

2

This is a book about being a seed planter.

1 Corinthians 3:8
The one who plants and the one who waters work together with the same purpose. And both will be rewarded for their own hard work.

So, this is about ministering, not preaching. It is about understanding that sometimes you are planting seeds and sometimes you are watering them. It is about letting people know that you accept them just as they are; where they are. It is about approaching them from the direction *they* need. It is about planting seeds. Jesus is love and acceptance. He hates sin but loves the sinner. As His disciples, we have to learn how to separate the sin from the sinner, minister to the *person* while rejecting the sin.

But what exactly is ministry?

Ministry is more than teaching or preaching, it is servitude to others. It is serving others just as Jesus served people. It is showing others the face of Jesus, introducing them to Him, through ourselves and our own actions. It is our job as Christians to minister to others, to lead others to Christ. However, sometimes "closing the sale," so to speak, is not and should not be the primary goal. Jesus wanted to save everyone while He walked the earth, but not everyone turned away from the world to follow Him. Still, He reached out to them, still loved them, still kept showing them love and compassion. Sometimes it is our job to simply plant the seed, to open the window.

The ideas here are just a few ways that you can minister to others. Some may have immediate results while others may plant a seed. But the goal here is to bring Jesus into the equation, to make the introduction (and foster the relationship if you are able). So, this little book is just a start. Some of these ideas cost money, some cost some time and some will cost you a little pride. In the end, though you will not only enrich the life of those you minister to, but also enrich your own relationship with Christ. There are many, many ways to minister to others and I hope that you will be inspired by this list and come up with your own unique ways to show God's love to people and introduce them to Jesus.

One last thing I want to note. These things open doors for you to show people the face of Jesus. Sometimes your kind act will soften someone's heart for someone else to water the seed, allowing them to hear God speak to their spirit. Other times, you will follow through once that door is open. Let them know that the glow about you, your radiant smile and your gentle heart come from Christ. Always, always give Him the glory! When He truly is a part of you, has filled you with His spirit, referring to Him and the works He has done in your life is as natural as breathing. It is a natural for you to refer to Jesus as it is for you to refer to your husband or wife or best friend.

So, some of these open the door for others to complete the work and some allow you to follow through with sharing Jesus. Still others are more direct. But there is something for everyone here. You should be able to find at least one or two things that you can do – and do today.

I have arranged this book into twelve different areas where you can plant seeds. Of course, most of the suggestions are not bound to just one area, but that is up to you to apply these things to your own life in your own way. I hope that this sparks ideas and inspiration in you, compelling you to go and reach out to others. That is our mission as members of the body of Christ. It is our goal. It is our *responsibility*.

Are you up for it?

God bless you!

2

## PLANTING SEEDS AT CHURCH

**1. Don't let the new wear off of your church, Bible study, Sunday school or cell group members.**

So many times people come to a new church or join a Bible study group and are greeted so warmly. Everyone wants to talk to them, they are like rockstars. They honeymoon for a while; then one day it stops. People stop talking to them, they may even be ignored. People stop reaching out and eventually, they fade into the woodwork.

It is easy to make a fuss over new church or Bible study group members when they are shiny and new, but once the new wears off, much of the ministry goes too. Don't let this happen on your watch! Reach out to new members, sure, but take the time to reach out to established "non-honeymooning" members too.

## 2. Seek to understand.

Everyone is different. Each person has his or her own set of issues, things they are going through – and each will respond in their own unique way. Seek to understand the people with whom you come into contact. Talk to them; try to understand where they are coming from and why they act as they do. This is one I try to do because I have been misunderstood.

My Asperger's makes me less socially adept and I tend to be quiet and shy. Most people don't understand that and they take my actions to be arrogant, stuck up and aloof. They don't take the time to understand that my condition makes me the way that I am and if they would just get to know me they would find I am warm, funny and kind (my husband tells me this). So before you jump to conclusions about someone, seek to understand them.

## 3. Get to know <u>them</u>.

The best way to minister to someone, to show them the face of Jesus, is to get to know <u>them</u>. People like to feel special and when you take the time to get to know them, you are showing them that they are worth knowing – they are special. Ask them about their work, where they grew up, what they like to do. When I have known someone for a little while, I will ask them what their favorite food is and what their favorite color is.

You can also learn these little things by just listening to them when they talk. Listen to the things that they say and you can learn a lot. The key is to apply what you learn about that person and let them know that you have taken the time to get to know who they really are.

### 4. Meet them wherever they are.

People are not typically born holy. We are all sinners. But in order to reach someone, you have to be prepared to meet them right where they are. That does not mean that you condone sinful behavior, but it does mean that you do not demand someone meet certain standards before you share with them that Jesus loves them and wants a better life for them.

Many times God will put a person as far down as they can go, breaking them, because when you have hit rock bottom, the only way you can look is up. That is when many people will reach for God. When you meet them where they are, understand that you are not the one reaching them, God is using you and He is reaching out to them. You are the vessel He uses. If they are receptive, He will work in them and change them. But you have to plant that seed.

### 5. Join a prayer group (email, forum, cell group, etc.) and pray for the prayer requests.

Intercessory prayer is powerful. You have to come to God having forgiven those who have wronged you and ask His forgiveness, but once the slate is clean, your prayers raised for others can have a true impact. Yet quite often we promise to pray for someone but fail to follow through. Make a list of people to pray for if you have to, or pray for them right there. Do whatever you need to do in order to make your promise of prayer a reality.

## 6. Donate money or supplies to the Sunday school class at your church (even if you don't have a child in SS)

When you see craft supplies on sale at your favorite store, pick up some for your church's Sunday school class. You can also pick up toys for the nursery. Bless the children of your church, the next generation of believers, by giving to support their spiritual education and growth.

If you donate movies or books, make certain that their message is Biblically sound and appropriate for young, growing Christians. You can even do little things like supplying ink pens or other supplies or bringing some extra Bibles in case someone forgets theirs or doesn't have one.

## 7. Volunteer in your church

We are a part of the body of Christ. That is why it is very important to not only attend church regularly, but also to be involved in your church. Volunteering in your church serves several areas,

> 1) it keeps you connected to your church family,

> 2) it helps the church, staff and pastor and

> 3) it gives you the opportunity to inspire and influence others.

Now, don't expect to walk into a church and be appointed in a leadership position. In fact, if that happens, be cautious.

Typically, a pastor will have you participate or counsel you, have you go through the membership classes and attend church for a while (sometimes quite a while) before placing you in a leadership position. Remember, as a leader you are setting an example for the rest of the congregation.

You are setting a standard for them to follow. You don't want to lead them astray, even if it is unintentional. If you really feel God as led you to a leadership position, submit to the authority and wisdom of your pastor and wait if he feels that is best.

## 8. Form a playgroup/Bible study with other moms

If you have children, form a Bible study with other moms and turn it into a playgroup for the children. You can each take turns having one mom watch the kids while the other moms discuss the Bible study. You can pray, worship, share praise reports and study the Word together.

Older children may even enjoy their own Bible study. Moms can rotate, each taking turns to read a story and supervise a related craft with the children. This can be an encouraging, uplifting and joyful experience.

9. **Give small, inexpensive gifts to Sunday school, nursery and other staff members.**

There are many great ideas for inexpensive gifts that you can give to your church staff to show appreciation. Give a $5 gift card to a coffee shop or restaurant. Pick up a book or CD with inspirational music.

Another great idea is a desk calendar with Bible verses for each day. If they have children, offer to babysit while they run errands, go shopping or have a date night with their significant other. Cook a meal or bake some cookies (but make sure they aren't on a diet). If you get creative, you can come up with many great ideas and it shows the staff that you appreciate all that they do.

# 3

# PLANTING SEEDS IN STRANGERS

## 10. Smile and speak.

Sometimes you can make someone's day by simply speaking or even just smiling at them. People want to know that they are not invisible, that they are special and worth recognizing. By speaking to them, acknowledging them, you are saying to them, "You are not invisible. You are special. You are worth recognizing."

This can also open doors for later ministry where you share scripture with them. But don't fall into the trap of believing that strangers don't matter. You never know what that person is experiencing or what they are feeling. One smile, one "Good morning" could be what makes a difference for them. You also don't know when you might see them again.

## 11. Let someone go ahead of you in the checkout line.

I enjoy doing this one pretty routinely. One of the grocery stores I go to is known for its extremely long checkout lines. I will let someone go ahead of me, then start a conversation. Being an Aspie, I am pretty lousy with small talk, so I have a few "scripts" I keep in my head to act as conversation starters.

Just the other day, I allowed a woman ahead of me and we started talking about how the media skews our thinking about what is beautiful by posting celebrities without their makeup and plastering on the cover photos of celebrities who have become overweight or have cellulite.

The man ahead of her chimed in and so did the cashier. I mentioned that our media is essentially an educational system and they agreed. I told them that my husband and I don't watch much TV (we don't have cable), but we do watch movies that we rent from Christian Cinema.

They asked what that was and I told them it has Christian movies and family friendly movies. They asked for the URL so I gave it to them. A seed planted.

## 12. Give a compliment – sincerely.

It doesn't cost anything to say something nice to someone. When you see someone, say something nice to them. Tell them they did a good job or are doing a good job. If you encounter a clerk in a store or a waitress in a restaurant who gives you exceptional service, tell them. Just look for the positive in people and compliment the good things. This can often lead to conversations that lead to your sharing Jesus with someone.

**13. When you give away things you don't use, or you "freecycle," drop a card in the bag or box with scripture.**

Freecycle.org is an online community where people give away "freecycle" things they don't use or want. Many communities and cities have a Freecycle group. If you do this type of thing, when you give something away, drop a small business card with a Bible verse printed on it. You can also write a little note to the person, "I hope you like this <item>. God bless you." Sign your name and include a verse underneath. You can even just give the book, chapter and verse. It is just a gesture to encourage and to plant a seed.

**14. Leave a personal note or card when you tip at a restaurant.**

Print some business cards (you can do it on your own printer) that have a Bible verse or something encouraging on them. When you leave your tip at a restaurant, leave the card. You can also leave a little note. If the waiter was especially helpful and friendly, compliment that. You can also write a note to the manager or tell the manager about your exceptional service.

## 15. Let God guide you and listen to Him.

OK, this isn't as specific as most of the others, but it is just as important – if not more so. See, God will let you know what people need. Have you ever had an overwhelming urge to talk to someone, even a complete stranger? Have you ever felt like you had to call someone and when you did you found out that they really needed to hear from you? God speaks to our spirit and directs us in the ways that we can best minister to others. We just have to be still and listen, then obey when He prompts us.

## 16. Do something nice or show a kindness towards someone you don't know.

Some people forget that there is a whole world beyond the people that they know. In that world, there are strangers who need to know the love of God. You don't have to know someone do to something nice for them or to show them kindness. Hebrews 13:1-2 "Let love of the brethren continue. Do not neglect to show hospitality to strangers, for by this some have entertained angels without knowing it." (New American Standard).

Feed a hungry person, clothe a cold person, yes, but also open a door for someone who has their hands full. Let someone go ahead of you in the checkout line at the store. Smile and wish someone a good day. It may not seem like much to you, but to someone it could mean all the difference. Every kindness extended to someone has to potential to soften their heart a little more.

## 17. Say Thank You

Now many people will probably think that this shouldn't be mentioned, but please hear me out. I have two reasons for including this as a way to minister to others. First, courtesy is dying. People just aren't as courteous as they used to be and it is getting worse. Second, mumbling thank you as you dig in your bag or have your mind on your next task is not what I am talking about here. I am talking about *looking* at the person, smiling and giving them a heart-felt, *sincere*, "Thank you."

I have Asperger's syndrome and eye contact is very difficult for me. However, I try to at least make eye contact, even if for the briefest of moments and I make sure I am smiling when I do it. Often I include something extra, whether it is telling a clerk at a store that they are doing a good job, or telling the bus driver to have a great day and be safe. If you are going to say thank you, give them the whole package.

4

# PLANTING SEEDS THAT HEAL

## 18. Look at the heart, not the circumstances.

Jesus spent time with thieves, prostitutes, murders and other characters that might be considered "unsuitable" company for Christians. However, He saw the value in each and every one, regardless of what they were doing or where they were in life. He saw everyone as having value and worth saving. So don't go thinking that you are too bad to get into Heaven or too good to minister to someone because they don't dress nice or they smell or they do things that are "un-Christian" because those are the very people we should be reaching out to – the lost. And they all deserve to learn about Jesus and meet Him.

## 19. Accept an outcast.

Look around for people who are not in the "in-crowd" and befriend them. I was always the outcast and I learned a deep appreciation for being accepted. Because of this, I began to reach out to other outcasts when I was in school and I met some of the most interesting and funny people! Unfortunately, outcasts can exist anywhere: school, the workplace, even families. They aren't difficult to spot, though, just look for the person who keeps to himself and reach out.

Be prepared, though, they may be suspicious at first because they are not accustomed to having people reach out to them. But if you go gently and are patient, you will find that many of these outcasts are delightfully different – and terribly misunderstood. Just accept them as they are.

### 20. Don't try to change people (leave it to God).

Acceptance has great power. If you have ever heard the saying, "You can lead a horse to water, but you can't make him drink" then you understand that you can't change people. But accepting them where they are without trying to *change* them can soften them to receive the change that God will put in their hearts. Then you can step up to offer support and help.

As God begins to work in them, you may feel led to lead them to scriptural references, or maybe it is someone else's calling to do that – you have to accept that as well. Just know that God will shine the light on the dark areas. The changes are between that person and God. We can't change anyone but ourselves and even then we have to ask Jesus for help.

## 21. Make someone laugh.

I once met a young man on the subway who had mastered this skill. As we were waiting on the platform for the train, he turned to me and said, "Hi. I am in the Special Olympics." I congratulated him and we began talking. His name is David.

David uses humor to break through the barriers that can occur when someone is "mentally challenged" (I am sorry if this offends, I don't know the politically correct term for this) because people often fear what they don't understand. He used silly jokes and some funny pranks to make people see past his challenges and see him.

By the time he got off of the train, the entire section of the car was smiling. We had all been talking to and laughing with David on our commute home.

Laughter is cleansing and healing so making someone laugh is a great way to minister to them. You can share a funny story, tell a joke "preferably clean" or just share in the joy of living with them. A good site for finding clean jokes is Beliefnet's Joke of the Day (http://www.beliefnet.com/Entertainment/Joke-of-the-Day/Daily-Joke.aspx). They have some really cute, funny, clean jokes that are sure to elicit a chuckle or two – and help you minister to someone by raising their spirits.

## 22. Admit when you make mistakes and apologize.

Pride will get you into a lot of trouble and it will stunt your spiritual growth. Not admitting mistakes and not apologizing when you should are two great, big, glaring signs of pride. Pride is also often rooted in rebellion. God honors humility and obedience.

When you humble yourself and say, "I made a mistake," and then you genuinely apologize, you are honoring God, pleasing Him. It may be a little difficult at first, but once you do it a few times it gets easier. Humility is a great tool for planting seeds. Obedience makes the job easier and God wants us to be obedient to Him. He will bless you for your obedience.

As followers of Christ, we are His representatives here on Earth. People (should) see Him through us. We are setting examples for others to follow. This is a big, important job and there is room for neither pride nor rebellion.

## 23. Invite them to church.

If you saw a great movie, you would want to tell your friends about it, maybe even take them to it, right? So why is it that we balk at inviting people to church or even sharing the Word with them? Are you afraid that you won't "fit in" with those people any longer?

When you repent, when you are baptized, when you are filled with the Holy Ghost, you become one of His. You become "set apart." You receive something this world can never give you and become something this world can never make you. It is awesome, it is exciting and it is supposed to be shared. So what are you waiting for? Invite people to church so that they can experience what you have, what you are. The worst they can do is decline the invitation.

## 24. Give someone a book that touched your life.

I am an avid reader. I am careful about what I read, what I allow to enter my mind and my spirit. I read some Christian fiction, but I really enjoy the non-fiction books on spiritual warfare and Godly living. I absolutely LOVE the Pentecostal Publishing House (http://pentecostalpublishing.com), they have an exceptional selection of books, music and Bible study materials (and their prices are great).

Quite often, after I read a book that really has a profound effect on me, I will pass it on to someone else. To be completely honest, if it is a book I really like, I will buy an additional copy for "Stephanie's Library." That way, if the person I lend it to really likes it, I can just give it to them.

## 25. Tell someone they are very special.

People need to feel special, *all* people, not just children. Let someone know that you think they are special. Thank God for them (and let them hear you)! Let them know that they have special gifts, a special purpose, that God created them as a special being.

Don't ever take it for granted that someone "just knows." Let them know. You can tell them, say something nice about them in front of others or give them a card or letter that expresses how special they are. You can demonstrate, but the *words* are very important.

## 26. Forgive

Forgiveness seems to be a difficult thing for many people to do. Granted, forgiveness really helps you more than it does the other person in many cases, but it is vital to all parties involved just the same. I have struggled to understand what forgiveness feels like. I have come to the conclusion, mostly due to the guidance of my very Godly, wise husband, that true forgiveness means that you no longer feel animosity towards the person, you don't want revenge; don't want them to "pay" for what they have done.

That is hard. True forgiveness means that you have to find that Godly love for the person or people who wronged you and love them like Christ loves us. After all, He died for *all* of us, even the ones who hurt us.

## 27. Give love even when you don't get it back.

The world is full of people who don't like us and certainly don't love us. As Christians, though, we are to love everyone – even when they don't love us in return.

Now, I am not talking about the love that most people show, they kind that holds grudges and sets limits and is guided by messy emotions. No, I am talking about a Christ-like love, a love that does not waver, that is kind and gentle. It does not mean that you have to let people run over you and take advantage of you, but it does mean that you are kind and have a forgiving heart.

I was in a situation at work where I was treated very badly by some people, mainly due to my Asperger's and their lack of understanding. Even when they were at their cruelest, I strove to remain kind and friendly. I offered help when it was needed, was encouraging and friendly. They certainly did not return the gestures, but I gave that love not expecting anything in return.

5

# PLANTING SEEDS THAT ENCOURAGE

## 28. Let them know you care.

There are many ways you can let a person know that you care. You can ask them how they are, and sincerely want to know. You can put a hand on their shoulder when words just aren't enough. You can pass by and give them a thumbs up when they are going through a difficult time. The possibilities are endless. I had a coworker, a friend who was going through a very difficult time there, we both were. There was some unfair treatment and the leadership was not kind at all.

One day I was in a small shop and saw a silly plaque. It said something like "Warning! I have flying monkeys and I'm not afraid the use them!" I bought it for her and put the bag on her chair while she was away from her desk. Of course, she knew exactly who got it for her and she loved it. She still has it on her desk, displayed where all can see – and she can be encouraged when things are difficult.

## 29. Share the scriptures with someone.

The Bible is full of encouraging scripture; you probably have some of your own favorites. Share those verses with someone. If you know of someone who is going through a difficult time, share a verse with them. You can approach them and say something like, "I know you are going through a difficult time and I just wanted to share a Bible verse with you that has always brought me comfort in times like this."

Sometimes I send it via email and other times I go straight to the person and tell them face to face. Sharing one word can sometimes lead that person to the exploration of the Bible and other scripture. Still, just letting them know that you care and you share with them plants a wonderful seed.

## 30. Use your blog or website to publish encouraging words and help others find Jesus

Your blog or website can be a powerful tool to encourage, witness and plant seeds. Talk about your favorite Bible verses, the ways that God is working in your life and your insights into various situations. Give your efforts to God, pray for guidance and allow Him to lead you as you write. When you write for God, seeking to reach those who need encouragement, He will bless your efforts. My blog, TheChristianAspie.com is popular and has many regular visitors, yet I have not formally advertised it. I share it on my Facebook and Twitter and sometimes in the occasional forum, but the readership has grown pretty much on its own. God is leading these hungry people to His words.

## 31. Share your testimony

Sharing your testimony can inspire and encourage others who may feel lost, alone, hopeless, discouraged or who are seeking for something they cannot identify (God). When you share your testimony, though, don't expect the earth to move and angels to sing. Sometimes the person will get excited and want to know more, want what you have (God).

Other times, though, they will smile, they may seem to shrug off the experience or even claim it to be coincidence. They may try to downplay the awesome ways that God moves in your life. Don't back down. Don't argue with them, but just simply state you KNOW it is God in your life. Then let it go. Even if they don't seem to accept it at the time, the seed has been planted.

## 32. Let someone know that you believe in them.

It feels good when someone believes in you, doesn't it? When you face an insurmountable challenge (even if it is just getting out of bed and facing the day) it helps to know that you are not along, that someone believes you can do it. Give people that encouragement, that strength.

During your morning prayers, ask God to place people in your path whom you can encourage and help. Ask Him to help you identify and discern those who need to hear those simple words, "I believe in you."

## 33. Commend someone when they do a good job.

Too often these days people are too busy to compliment others, to tell them that they are doing a good job. The words are so simple, "You are doing a good job." The next time you are at a store, talking to your kids, spending time with your spouse, working with a co-worker, just say those words. *Everyone* can benefit from some kind words and knowing that they are doing a good job.

Once I was in a store and witnessed a customer being very rude, even abusive, to a young clerk. The young woman kept her cool, remained polite and professional even though the man was yelling at her and calling her names. She never raised her voice. I walked over to her and asked her a question about a product. The man stormed out. I then told her what a good job she did handing him. Her hands were shaking as she rung me up, but she was obviously encouraged by the positivity.

After I left, I wrote a letter to her company commending her for her professionalism and courtesy in the situation. People need to know when they are doing something right – we are usually so quick to point out when they are doing something wrong, aren't we?

## 34. Reach out to people even when they aren't sick or distressed.

Sure you help the elderly lady with her groceries. Of course you take soup to the ill mother of three or pray with the grieving widower. But what about the people who don't have apparent adversities in their lives? What about them? Keep in mind that some people may have the appearance that nothing is "wrong" in their lives when the complete opposite is true. Then again, even people who don't appear to need encouragement can still use it. The can still benefit from seeds planted.

### 35. Reach out to people who are shy and are ignored/forgotten

This is something that is very close to me because I am shy and tend to be ignored. My Asperger's makes me socially awkward. I tend to retreat. Because I don't feel like I fit in most places, it means a lot when someone takes the time to reach out to me. If you are shy or socially awkward, you know what I mean. I don't mean someone putting the spotlight on me, just noticing me, talking to me and being kind.

So quietly reach out to people who are shy, who seem ignored or forgotten. Show interest in them, genuine interest. Let them know that you care. Let them know that they matter. That can make all the difference to someone who feels left out and alone in the world.

### 36. Post encouraging words and scripture on your social media profiles

Your FaceBook, MySpace, Twitter and other social media profiles allow you to potentially reach hundreds, if not thousands, of people. Many of those people are hungry and in need of encouragement. Post encouraging words and scripture on your profiles. Realize, though, that you also have to back it up with appropriate behavior. If you post a Bible verse on your profile one day and swear at someone the next, you have just undermined your credibility. If you are going to talk the talk, then you need to walk the walk as well. Remember, others are watching you, everything you do. They will emulate you. Where do you want to lead them?

6

## PLANTING SEEDS AT WORK

### 37. Be encouraging.

This can mean simply calling someone who is going through a tough time and asking them how they are doing. It can mean sending an email with a special Bible verse or quote or poem of just a note to say "I care." Being encouraging does not have to be elaborate, you just have to care. Ministry is more than telling people about Jesus, it's about *showing* them Jesus. Teaching is great and very necessary, but if you don't back it up with the appropriate actions, you are going to lose credibility. In other words, walk the talk.

### 38. Ask how they are (and really listen to their reply).

One thing that really bothers me is that most people will say, "How are you?" and either never waits for the answer or they are not interested in the answer (they want you to just say "fine."). On top of that, they expect you to ask them how they are!

31

And the whole charade plays out again. It is really silly, asking questions that you don't really want the answers to, but people do it every day.

So, one of the great ways to minister to someone is to ask them how they are, and *mean* it. Let them know that you are truly interested in how they are doing. Ask follow up questions, look at them; give them your undivided attention.

## 39. Share a Bible verse.

I know plenty of non-churchgoing people. Some I work with or have worked with in the past. Some claim to have problems with the church (really just excuses not to go, but I don't say that) and some say they "are spiritual, not religious" (which means they don't know what to believe and they don't feel motivated to explore further). Some have beliefs that are different from mine.

But one thing that they all respond to is scripture. When someone is having a bad day or has been going through a difficult time, I will send them a scripture with a note, "Praying for you." And they always write back that it was just what they needed.

I find Bible verses at a couple of web sites (because they are very easily searchable to keyword). The radio station K-LOVE (www.klove.com) has an "Encouraging Word" every day on their website.

If you subscribe to it, you will receive it in your email inbox. I can't tell you how many times I have opened that precious email and felt God talking directly to me through the words.

I also use BibleGateway
(http://www.biblegateway.com) because I can do a
keyword search and find scripture specific to the
situation.

## 40. If someone is struggling (even if they drop something) stop and help them.

It takes just a moment to reach out a helping hand
to someone. If someone drops something, help
them pick it up. Anywhere you see a need, see
someone who needs help, step up, reach out a hand
and help. If someone is having difficulty with a
project, see if you can help them.

I have people at my former place of employment
who still call me for help on things. I made myself
available to help them and they still reach out to
me. It is my opportunity to minister to them, to
show them Jesus.

## 41. At work, keep a sweater handy in case someone gets cold – you can lend it to them.

I am not a cold natured person, but I do keep a
sweater in my office. It is just habit and sometimes
I do need it when the weather unexpectedly
changes or I feel ill. But I realized that many people
get very cold at work. Sometimes they have an
officemate who keeps the AC on full blast and
other times they have to attend a meeting in an ice
cold conference room. Whatever the case, I found
that keeping an extra sweater in my office gives me
the opportunity to witness to others.

In my case, it opens doors for conversation and
brings them into my office where I have scripture

posted on my cabinets and my Bible on my desk. They are exposed to kindness and one word can lead to another which can lead to witnessing to them.

## 42. Share your lunch with someone who forgot theirs.

This may seem trivial, but when we extend kindness to others it makes an impact. If someone forgets their lunch or doesn't have money for lunch, give them part of yours. If you have the means, get them something. Just the act of extending that care and kindness can soften hearts for God's word and show them Christian love.

## 43. Support your leadership (even if you don't always agree with them)

We don't always agree with our leadership. Sometimes they are cruel. Sometimes they are unethical. However, they are always the authority figure that God has placed over us – yes, even those who are not Godly. Submitting to that authority is submitting to God's authority.

That does not mean that you must engage in any illegal, unethical, abusive or ungodly activities, but you must give that authority a certain degree of respect because God placed you in that situation.

I was once in a situation where my leadership was cruel and abusive – to me as well as other employees. I did not engage in their behavior, but I did respect the people. I was courteous and professional. And I prayed for them. Through this experience and my submission to God's authority in the matter, I not only received a better job, but the leader was removed from her position so she was no longer able to abuse the remaining employees.

No matter the situation, know that God is working in it. Pray for the situation and for the people involved (even the leadership). Pray for discernment and wisdom in dealing with the people, pray for a good attitude and pray for the ability to learn well the lesson that God is giving you.

## 44. Have a lunch hour Bible study at work

A lunch hour Bible study is a great way to fellowship, increase your Biblical knowledge and witness to others. Realistically, in some workplaces you must be discrete; you may even need to hold the Bible study offsite in a neutral area such as a coffee shop or restaurant. But it is well worth it.

If you are willing to work around corporate restrictions that seek to inhibit Christian activities or even keep it out completely, God will honor your efforts. For some, your lunch hour Bible studies will be the only church they know.

## 45. Lead by following.

Leading is not about bossing people around. It is about empowering and encouraging people to excel. This is true on the job as well as in ministry. No one wants doctrine shoved down their throats and no one wants someone looking over their shoulder the entire time they are working.

So, lead by example, by stepping back and letting people step up. You maintain your authority much more effectively by empowering your people to lead. After all isn't that what Jesus did when He washed His disciples' feet?

## 46. Show them Jesus through your own example

Some people may roll their eyes when they see the popular WWJD – What Would Jesus Do? Actually, it is a great way to live. Thinking about what Jesus would do in situations and using that as a guide for your decisions will help you make wise decisions. This means acting as Jesus would – with gentleness and love, but unwavering in your commitment to God's word.

You may be the only Jesus that some people see. You may be the first contact with Jesus that some people have. What kind of an impression are you making?

7

# PLANTING SEEDS IN YOUR COMMUNITY

### 47. Offer to help.

This one is pretty general, but very effective. If you see someone who needs help, give it to them. Once I was walking across the parking lot after shopping. An elderly woman was putting her bags into her car and dropped one. The contents rolled all over the lot. I parked my cart and helped her gather her things and put them back in the bag. She was very grateful and thanked me several times.

I try to offer my help when I see someone struggling with something or when they appear to need assistance. Sometimes they say yes and sometimes they say no. But I do try.

Matthew 25:31-40 ~ [34] "Then the King will say to those on His right, 'Come, you who are blessed of My Father, inherit the kingdom prepared for you from the foundation of the world. [35] For I was hungry, and you gave Me *something* to eat; I was thirsty, and you gave Me *something* to drink; I was a stranger, and you invited Me in; [36] naked, and you clothed Me; I was sick, and you visited Me; I was in prison, and you came to Me.' [37] Then the righteous will answer Him, 'Lord, when did we see You hungry, and feed You, or thirsty, and give You *something* to drink? [38] And when did we see You a stranger, and invite You in, or naked, and clothe You? [39] When did we see You sick, or in prison, and come to You?' [40] The King will answer and say to them, 'Truly I say to you, to the extent that you did it to one of these brothers of Mine, *even* the least *of them*, you did it to Me.'

## 48. Volunteer.

Giving yourself, giving your time and talents to help others is a great way to show God to people. It may mean you have to get up a little earlier on Saturday or give up some of your leisure time, but when you give up, you "give up" (as in upwards – to God). You glorify God through your act of giving. I was surprised to find the small opportunities in my own community for volunteering. If you look and ask around, you could probably find some too. Even visiting people in a retirement home or state funded home (many have volunteer companion programs) give you the opportunity to show someone Jesus' face.

## 49. Cook a meal.

Many churches have a cooking ministry - and for a very good reason. Cooking for someone is one of the best ways to get close to a person. New parents, people who are moving, the bereaved, people who are ill and the elderly are just some of the people who could benefit from and would likely appreciate a home cooked meal. Simple crock pot meals are great, you don't have to do anything very fancy. Soup, stew, beans and rice, spaghetti and other quick, easy meals (I am from Louisiana, I have tons of easy, delicious, southern recipes!) are perfect for this type of ministry. Also, if you can provide something that freezes well, that is a bonus.

## 50. Do yard work – for someone else.

When I was growing up, my father would mow the grass every Saturday morning (we lived in the Deep South, so the grass needed mowing just about all year round). He would also go over and mow my aunt's yard (her husband, my uncle, was a quadriplegic – she had a lot going on). Then he would mow the single mom's yard next door and an elderly man's yard down the street. As a child, this was just how it was done in my world, but later, as I got older and more aware of the world, I realized how he was ministering to these people with such a simple act.

## 51. Visit with someone who may be alone or isolated.

Giving someone your time can be one of the best gifts you can give. Some people who may be isolated or alone might include the elderly, single mothers, stay at home moms, someone who is ill or someone who doesn't have any family living nearby. Just taking time to visit with someone is a good way to minister to them. Humans have an innate need to be social, to interact with other humans.

Although, some people need to be around people more than others, the need is still there is almost everyone. Even I need and desire to be around people sometimes, though not much. So many people, though, just don't have the time or they don't make the time. That is how the ones needing the company or interaction get hurt and the ones who are too busy have a lost opportunity to show the caring side of Christianity to someone.

## 52. Support Christian businesses and businesses that support Christian missions.

Christian businesses and businesses that support Christian ministries and missions are usually supported by generous donors and loyal patrons who believe in the cause. You may be surprised, if you look around, at the many different places that are Christian businesses and that support Christian endeavors.

Look into thrift stores and see if they are privately owned, or if they support something. You may be surprised. Many areas have Christian business directories and in many cities, the information is available online. If you are going to spend your money on something, it is better to spend it to further the works of those who are working for God.

## 53. Do "little things" to help out. If a dog gets into your neighbor's garbage, pick it up for them or help them pick it up.

Many times, we see things that need to be done, people who could use a little help, but we think,

"Oh, it's just a little thing. It's no big deal." And we walk on.

What if we stop and do that "little thing that is no big deal?" It could make a big difference in someone's life. If a dog gets into your neighbor's garbage, pick it up – even if it isn't your dog or your garbage. If you see someone doing something just stop, pitch in and help. This is a great way to start a conversation, even witness to them. All it takes is a little time and a sincere smile.

## 54. Thank the people in your community who work to make it better (policemen, firemen, garbage men, mailmen, etc.)

When was the last time you thanked the men who collect your garbage on trash day? Take the time to thank those who work in your community to make it better and safer. Give a thank you card and include a gift card or certificate (some people may be wary of baked goods or food). You can also give Christmas ornaments or bookmarks and other small, thoughtful gifts.

8

# PLANTING SEEDS IN UNEXPECTED PLACES

**55. Take your shopping cart to the cart corral or back up to the store instead of leaving it sitting in the parking lot.**

Now, you may do this on a regular basis and if that is the case, good for you! However, many, many people do not. This is a small, simple act that shows respect. You can even take it a step farther by offering to return someone else's cart as well as your own. Something so simple can go a long way.

**56. Thank your public transportation operator (bus, subway, train, etc.)**

If you take public transportation such as the bus or train, thank the operator. For instance, when you board the bus, greet them with a smile and a friendly hello. Sometimes you may be met with stony silence, but do it anyway. Some operators are not accustomed to patrons speaking to them. But greet them and when you leave, wish them a nice day and tell them thank you.

I take a bus when I commute in to Washington, D.C. each day. When I get on the bus in the morning I always greet the driver. When I get off the bus, I always thank them. If it is raining, I tell them to be careful. On Fridays, I wish them a good weekend. I do the same for the afternoon driver. It doesn't take any of my time, doesn't cost anything, but you can tell that it makes them feel good, and that is what it is all about.

**57. Write a letter to a person's manager or the company, complimenting them for great service, customer service, etc.**

I love doing this! All too often, we are quick to complain about a person, but rarely do we take the time to compliment someone to their manager or company they work for.

With so many companies having an online presence now, it is easy to log on and send a note to the company telling them about an exemplary employee or outstanding service you have received. Make certain that you name names, give specific dates and times and offer details.

If you write a letter to send in the mail, send a copy to the company, manager and the employee if you have enough information to send it to their place of employment. Another way to deliver a letter is in person. The important thing is that you do it.

## 58. Find the good in someone and point it out to them.

It is easy to find the bad in people, but look for the good. When you find something that is good about someone, they do their job well, have a great smile or are easy to talk to, let them know. You never know when you will make someone's day by doing so.

I once met a young man who had a great smile. It wasn't perfect or dazzling. In fact, his teeth were a little crooked. But when he smiled, his whole face lit up, his eyes danced and you just had to smile too. It was a truly beautiful, sincere smile. So I told him.

He was gracious enough, but humble. Later, though, he sent me a note telling me that my telling him that meant so much to him because he always felt self conscious about his smile. He said it really made his day. See, you never know.

## 59. Keep some $5 and $10 gift cards to nearby food establishments like McDonald's and others to hand out to people who are homeless and hungry.

I try to do this whenever I can. There are a lot of homeless and hungry people in D.C. I encounter them daily when I work. They are at the subway stations and on the street. What I try to do is keep these gift cards with me and when I see someone who is hungry or homeless, I give one to them. Most of the time they are very well received and appreciated.

Many different places have gift cards. If you see people in certain areas, find places that are economical and close to get the cards.

McDonald's is a very popular restaurant and you can find them almost anywhere. They are really good because they have dollar menu items. When you get the cards, keep these things in mind. Keep it simple, close in proximity and inexpensive.

## 60. Be a good tipper with a little flair.

Add a brief, personal note, thanking them and sharing a favorite scripture. One Saturday, my husband, daughter and I had breakfast at a popular restaurant. We had terrible service. It was really awful. We had to wait for more than a half an hour while we watched people who had arrived after us receive their food, finish and leave.

When we got our food, most of it was cold. My toast and fried eggs were stone cold, but I did not want to wait another half hour to get more so I choked it down.

Our server knew he had messed up and he apologized several times. He was young and seemed inexperienced. There was conversation about leaving a tip – some wanted to and others did not. I wanted to, though, and since I was paying, <smile> I left one.

It was about ten percent, but I also left a note (I keep a small note pad and pen with me) that I hope encouraged him. It said something to the effect of "Be encouraged, this is a learning experience. You will do better next time, have a nice day." And I drew a smiley face.

## 61. Talk to a child and show you value what they say, let them know you are listening

Children have important things to say too. Sometimes adults listen, but all too often, they nod, but never really hear them. You might be surprised if you stop and take the time to actually listen to a child. And you just might make their day. The best thing is that you don't even have to be a "kid person" to do this. It is quite easy.

When a child is talking to you, ask questions just as you would anyone else. If your friend was reading a book, you would ask what it was about, what they like about it, what they don't like. You can talk to a child the same way. You can even talk about things going on in their world, at school, with their friends, anything.

The best thing you can ask is "What do you think about that?" When they tell you, ask questions to understand better why the feel the way they do. Don't condemn, just ask and discuss. You might be surprised and you just might learn something.

## 62. If the person in the checkout line ahead of you is short on cash, help them out.

Sometimes God puts us in the paths of people who need help, He sets us up to make the decision to help or walk on by. Which do you choose to do?

The next time you are in the checkout line at the grocery store and the person ahead of you has to put food back because they don't have enough, kindly, quietly and graciously help them out. You can pay for the item or give them a few dollars to make the total bill. Most of the time, this act will be very much appreciated. It is a small act of kindness that will go a long way. And God will bless you for it.

9

## PLANTING SEEDS IN FRIENDS

### 63. Pray for someone.

This may seem like a no-brainer, but it is a simple, effective way to minister to someone. You can pray with them if they are present, or you can pray for them if they are not accessible. Praying with them, so they know you are praying for them, ministers to them and they are consciously aware of what you are doing.

However, you can minister just as effectively if they don't know you are praying for them. In those cases, you are ministering to their spirit. They may not be consciously aware, but on a spiritual level, they will know and they will reap the benefits.

Don't hold your prayers for someone or discount private prayers, this is an important method of ministry. If they are present and receptive, offer to pray for them – then do it.

## 64. Be accessible.

One thing that is very apparent when we look at Jesus' life is how accessible He was and still is. "Come to Me, all you who labor and are heavy laden, and I will give you rest" (Matthew 11:28). Oh, and also, "But I said to you that you have seen Me and yet do not believe. All that the Father gives Me will come to Me and the one who comes to Me I will by no means cast out" (John 6:36). Powerful stuff. Jesus is totally accessible and as his disciples, we should be as well.

## 65. Write a note or card.

I am a big writer of notes and cards. I give cards to my children "just because" and they seem to really like it. Once I wrote a letter to each of my children, telling him or her how proud I was of them and how I know that they will make wise decisions. They have kept these letters like little treasures.

You can write notes, even a sticky note on the bathroom mirror can brighten someone's day. I have left notes on friends' cars, just to say hi. Include a favorite Bible verse, something appropriate for the situation, or if it a "just because" note, include one that you really like.

## 66. Give someone a flower.

I don't mean go out and buy a big fancy bouquet, although that is OK too. I mean pick up a potted flower plant or even a single flower and give it to the person. Flowers have a way of brightening an area and bringing life to it. They can lift a person's mood and be encouraging. I would love to see the old May Day traditions return where people decorated baskets and left them on people's doorsteps.

## 67. Hug.

I will admit, I am not much of a hugger. Asperger's makes it rather uncomfortable to hug much of the time – too much stimulation. But a well placed hug now and then can let someone know that you care, let them know you are there for them and the physical contact alone has powerful psychological benefits (according to several scientific studies). It might be best if you ask first if is OK to hug them, but if they say yes, go for it!

## 68. Buy someone lunch.

We have already visited a version of this, but now expand it. Buy a friend lunch, a coworker lunch, someone from church. It may turn into an opportunity to make a new friend and could open doors for witnessing to people.

This little act does not necessarily originate in the need for something to eat as in the other version. The need to be filled here is more social in nature. It is good to spend time with people and it is part of God's plan to reach out to others and lead them to him.

## 69. Ask, "What is your opinion?

We are all full of our own opinions, but when was the last time you asked someone for their opinion and genuinely wanted to hear their answer? We can learn a lot from people and the more you ask – and, more importantly, listen - the more you can learn. When you have a better understanding of what people believe and why they believe it, you can better help them find a real and lasting relationship with Christ.

## 70. When someone contacts you (calls, writes, emails), contact them back.

This is a very hard one for me! According to the research on Asperger's (and as you may recall, I have Asperger's), this is common. I do long for interpersonal relationships, but I am not very good at sustaining them.

I enjoy people, but prolonged social interactions exhaust me. I will write and email people, but sometimes it takes me a while. I don't really talk on the phone (I am "phone phobic" another Aspie trait that I am trying to overcome).

So, I will be practicing what I preach here, so to speak (I don't preach, but I will do as I say to do). When someone contacts you, write them back or contact them back. If time is an issue, set a certain amount of time for response, say five minutes to write and send an email, or ten minutes for a phone call (that seems like a long time for me, but I know other people who talk way longer on the phone).

It is also good to reach out to someone if you haven't heard from them in a while – that is sustaining a relationship, another thing I am working on personally.

## 71. Learn how to receive (not just give)

I love to give. I enjoy finding just the right gift for someone or giving them something that I know they need. I am not so great at receiving. It makes me uncomfortable when someone gives me something, I am never sure how to respond (I can thank the social awkwardness of Asperger's for this too). But, I am learning.

What I have learned from my wise, NT husband is that the best thing to do when someone gives you something is to smile and say, "Thank you." Sounds simple, huh? I thought it sounded too simple. But it works. Just be sincerely grateful for it and remember to thank them and that is surprisingly sufficient.

# 10

# PLANTING SEEDS THAT HELP

## 72. Fulfill a need.

You don't have to look very far to find people in need. People going through hard times due to job loss, financial problems, disaster and any number of other things have needs. If God has blessed you, you can help. Give clothing, food, money, whatever you can.

I prefer to give anonymously if at all possible. We don't have much, but God provides us with enough so instead of spending our money on something frivolous, we often use it to help someone. Why spend $50 on a fancy meal for two when you can feed a family for days with that money?

Go to a school or church and find families in need. You don't have to get names, just size, gender, maybe some preference of color or style, and what immediate needs they have (coats, shoes, etc.). Get the items and give them to the family or give them to the representative to give to the family (if you prefer to remain anonymous). It is a wonderful feeling to know that you truly helped someone.

## 73. Give up your seat on the bus (or subway).

For some people, this is a no-brainer. If you fit into this category, good for you. Your courtesy is very much appreciated. However, working in Washington, D.C. has taught me a few things. One of those things is that courtesy is sorely lacking in this world.

In February 2009, I broke my ankle and had to wear one of those orthopedic boots until it healed. I caught the subway and had to ride about 25 minutes to my stop. Now, there are certain seats on the subway that are designated for senior citizens and "the infirm" (like me at the time), yet young, healthy people would sit in those areas forcing those of us who should be sitting there to stand.

Many a day I had to ride the entire 25 minutes standing in a jostling subway car, trying to maintain my balance on one leg while perfectly healthy people (with two good legs) sat in those seats.

I will say that several times, military personnel would offer me their seats. I greatly appreciated that. But rarely would a civilian do it even though I was almost falling over.

With that being said, yes, it is a common courtesy, but it is, unfortunately, so rare these days to give your seat to someone else, it is definitely a way to minister to others.

## 74. Give someone a Bible.

What better gift can you give someone than to share the word of God with them? Give someone their very own Bible! When I give someone a Bible, I also like to write something in the front, include some of my favorite Bible verses, to make it more personal. Adding the verses also gives them a place to start if they are new to reading the Bible. The key is to get them into the pages.

You can find inexpensive Bibles in a couple of places. I really like the site ChristianBook.com (http://www.christianbook.com) because they have great prices, an easy to navigate website, great shipping and outstanding customer service. I can find New American Standard Bibles on there for around $5. When they have one of their awesome sales, it is even less!

Of course, AbeBooks (http://abebooks.com) is another site with good deals on Bibles too. If you shop around, you can pick up Bibles for just a little cash which means you can get more to give to more people. Spread the Word!

## 75. Comfort someone when they are sad

When a person is sad, it is often hard to find the right words to say. This is particularly true if you have never experienced what they are going through. Sometimes, you may not even know what they are going through; you just know that they are sad.

The way I see it, is a little different than how many people see it – from an Aspie perspective. I think that even though I may be experiencing the same thing as another person, I am not them – so how could I possible know how they feel?

My husband says you use empathy to *imagine*, but that is still imagining. My point here is, even if you don't know, or you are like me and can't imagine, you can still offer comfort. A hug, a sincere offer to help, letting them talk, are all ways that you can provide comfort. I am pretty good at just listening to someone and not inserting my own opinions. Sometimes just saying, "I am so sorry for what you are going through" works. You can share favorite Bible verses.

I am a photographer. There was a woman where I work who lost her sister. I took one of my photographs and used a software program to put a Bible verse (Matthew 28:20 "…and lo, I am with you always, even unto the end of the world.") on it. I printed it and put it in a frame. She loved it. Sometimes just showing someone you care is comfort enough.

## 76. Open your door to them.

I grew up in a home where my father was always bringing people home with him. They were hungry, homeless, down on their luck. We fed people, took blankets to the homeless down by the river, helped families find shelter. I still talk to some of these people today, years later.

I grew up with that same mentality. My door is open. People who know me know that they can come to me, call me anytime, day or night and I will be there. If someone came to me hungry, I would feed them.

Is your door open to your friends? Your neighbors? Do people feel comfortable coming to you or calling you for help? Open your heart and your door will follow.

### 77. Show grace and mercy.

This can be a hard one because people can be cruel. But, if you hold the love of God for them, you can rise above cruelty and abuse. I have had people over the years who were cruel, even brutal, to me. I have been through bullying, abuse, persecution, neglect. However, I have prayed hard and worked hard to forgive those people. And I pray that God will have mercy on them. I sincerely mean that.

The desire for vengeance if not profitable and it is just, plain wrong. It is definitely not Godly. I once had a boss who was very cruel to me. She was a bully and did things to me to try to force me to quit my job. She said terrible things to me to try to tear me down. I did not understand how mercy worked at the time. I am ashamed to say I did not pray for it for the woman. I just prayed for a resolution to the problem.

One day, she was fired without warning. I felt bad. I told some people (who knew what I had been going through with her) that she was fired and they were happy! I couldn't believe it. How could they be happy that a person lost their job? That just isn't a right way of thinking.

Later, I was faced with a similar situation, only worse. This time, I prayed that God would have mercy on the person. I was removed from under that person's leadership quite suddenly to a better position. I kept praying because other people were still under that leader. I kept asking for mercy. One day, quite suddenly, she was removed from her position – demoted to another position. But she did not lose her job. That is grace and mercy.

Animosity and a desire for vengeance will eat you up inside and separate you from God. If you have trouble in that area, pray for God to change it in you.

## 78. Clip coupons and give them to someone who could use them.

Many people use coupons. It is a great way to cut costs and save money. You can help by clipping coupons and giving them to someone who needs them. For instance, give a new mother diaper coupons, or someone on a budget coupons for food they normally purchase. If you are not certain, ask what coupons you can clip for them, or just put some in an envelope and leave it on their door as an anonymous surprise.

# 11

## PLANTING SEEDS ANONYMOUSLY

**79. Leave a Christian book in a public place for someone to find.**

When you read a great Christian book and you want to share it, give BookCrossing (http://www.bookcrossing.com) a shot. You register the book on the web site, print a label and place it in the book, then leave the book in a place where it can be found. The person who finds the book will be directed to the web site and encouraged to "log" the book so it can be tracked – then, of course left in another place to be found again. This is a great way to plant seeds.

**80. Have encouraging business cards printed with verses, websites, etc. and leave in public areas.**

Print your own business cards or go to a site such as Vistaprint (http://www.vistaprint.com) for free or very low cost cards. Add encouraging Bible verses. You may also include a website with information on salvation or getting closer to God.

Leave the cards in public areas or hand them out to people you meet.

## 81. Purchase extra items you find on sale and donate to a church, food bank or a charity.

Check to see if your church has a program for giving clothing, food or toiletry items to the needy. If so, pick up some items and donate them to the program. You can also donate to your local food bank or charities such as the Salvation Army (the Salvation Army has a wonderful program each Christmas where low income parents can "shop" for Christmas toys for their children for free).

Pick up some things on sale or use coupons and donate. There are always people who are in need. Remember Psalms 41: 1-2:

> [1] Blessed *is* he who considers the poor;
> The LORD will deliver him in time of trouble.
> [2] The LORD will preserve him and keep him alive,
> *And* he will be blessed on the earth;
> You will not deliver him to the will of his enemies.

## 82. Give old toys and clothes to people who can use it

When you clean out your closet or go through your children's old toys, instead of tossing them into the trash, keep the items that are in good shape and give them to people who can use them. You can give them to some thrift stores or to neighbors or to people you know can't afford such things. Give with a loving heart. Don't give with arrogance or pride because you have more than someone else. Give because you love God's people and you want to help.

## 83. Have business cards printed with contact info and include a verse.

When you meet people and give them your contact information, instead of writing it on a piece of paper, have some business cards printed with your name, phone number, email address and a favorite Bible verse. You can get inexpensive, or even free, business cards at Vistaprint (http://www.vistaprint.com).

# 12

# PLANTING SEEDS AT HOME

## 84. Email a song.

My husband does this for me and it makes my day. Find a song that has some special message for them or that you think will brighten their day. You can imbed videos from YouTube or send links, or you can send songs as a gift. Once they receive a song with your uplifting message attached, they will never hear it quite the same again. This simple ministry method has an added bonus of giving over and over again.

## 85. Listen, just listen.

Sometimes the kindest thing you can do for someone is to listen to them. People want to feel special, feel valued and when you listen to what they have to say, you are telling them that they are special and valued. This is a great way to minister to young people and children.

When in conversation, ask, "What do you think?" or "What are your views on this?" Watch their reaction; it is usually very nice to see. They will light up and start talking. If you are the one doing the talking, give them a chance to chime in. If they are upset or going through a difficult time, let them know that you are there to listen – and then do it. Offer advice only if asked, but give your ears and your attention freely.

## 86. Write a poem.

As a writer, this is an easy one for me, but I realize that some people may not feel that they have the ability to write, especially poetry. Don't let doubts stop you. Write what is on your heart. It doesn't have to be perfect; it doesn't even have to rhyme. Just write what you feel, or, better yet, what you feel God wants to tell them through you.

## 87. Give them space.

It is common to think of ministering to someone as being with them, touching them, talking to them, but sometimes the best way to minister to someone is by giving them their space. Let them know that you are there for them, that you are available and then back off. Let them do what they need to do, process, think, whatever. Come back to them later and you may see that you have fresh, new eyes too.

## 88. Minister to your family.

I have seen many people get all excited about ministering to other people, only to completely ignore and neglect their own families. Take the time to spend time with your family. Study the Bible together, pray together and make sure that God is the most important thing in your lives and at the center of your family.

Biblically, the priorities are first, God, then spouse, then children, then everyone and everything else (friends, family, job, etc.). Yes, you should be ministering to others and leading others to Christ, but you must keep your family at their Biblically designated level of importance. If they are working with you or pursuing their own ministries, that is even better. Just remember to not forget your family.

## 89. Send "just because" cards with encouraging messages.

You don't need a special occasion to send a card. Pick up a card and send it, "just because." There are many companies that make cards that are encouraging. One of my favorites is Blue Mountain (http://www.bluemountain.com). They have both ecards and print cards.

The print cards can be found in many popular stores that sell greeting cards. What I really like about this company is that they have cards that are spiritual with Bible verses and even sentiments that talk about God. The art work is also quite beautiful.

I like to choose the cards with uplifting messages, such as "I believe in you," or "you are special." You can send them to your children, your spouse, your friends, anyone who could use encouragement or a little boost. Don't look for a special occasion, the occasion is now.

## 90. Discipline your children.

One of the most loving things you can do for your children is to give the consequences for their actions. It is hard being the "bad guy" and imposing discipline on your children, but that is the Godly thing to do. I am neither condoning, nor am I condemning corporal punishment here .

But I am saying that when you child misses curfew (and they should have a curfew) or breaks the rules (yes, you should have rules in your home) then they should be held accountable and there should be consequences. It is your duty as a parent to train children up the way they should go. God mandates it.

## 91. Serve your spouse.

God tells us that we are to serve our spouse; it is noted in several verses in the Bible. Yes it is one of the most difficult concepts for some married couples to grasp.

In the book "7 Steps to a Godly Marriage" (http://www.smashwords.com/books/view/43908) there is an entire section on serving your spouse. This is a Biblical principle and indeed something to adopt if you want to have a Godly marriage. Now, this does not mean waiting on your spouse, hand and foot, allowing them to take advantage of you. It means caring for them and serving them in a loving way.

I serve my husband in many ways. When I cook dinner, I always make his plate and bring it to him. When he cooks, he makes my plate and brings it to me. I do things for him such as making sure that his clothes are clean, hung up and pressed (not always easy with a full time job that involves a 3 hour commute round trip). I encourage him and do my best to make our home as comfortable as possible.

He does the same for me. We take care of each other and we do it with love. Serving your spouse does not mean that you have ammunition to hold over their head and manipulate them. It means that you take care of your spouse and love them the way God says we should.

## 92. Learn the Word and pray for wisdom

When you read the Bible daily and pray for wisdom, you gain understanding that will benefit every aspect of your life. This will guide you as you minister to people on all levels and in all ways. Find a good plan that will guide you through the Bible in an organized way. If you can find a Bible study program that also has supplementation explaining the scripture, that is even more beneficial. I really like the Pentecostal Publishing House (http://pentecostalpublishinghouse.com) because they have a great selection, great prices and solid instruction.

# 13

# PLANTING SEEDS BY SERVING OTHERS

## 93. Visit a hospital

Just about any doctor will tell you that one of the best medicines for healing is caring interaction with others. It doesn't require a great deal of time or expense to volunteer at a hospital just visiting the patients. You can take an hour or so on Saturdays or a couple of mornings a week if you don't work. Just the simple act of sitting with someone, talking with them, showing them that you care about them means so much.

You can plant seeds by the simple act of giving your time, but you can often further that by sharing the Word as you visit. God's word will bring comfort to those who are alone, sick and scared.

## 94. Do someone else's chores for them

If you are in a household where everyone is assigned chores, take on someone else's for them, especially if they need the time for something else.

Help clean your church. If you see a neighbor doing yard work or taking the garbage to the curb, help them. This is about helping someone, going above and beyond, doing something unasked for and unexpected. When you see an opportunity, take it. Step up and do a chore for someone else.

## 95. Volunteer to mentor an at-risk child

Many schools have mentorship programs. You can give your time to a child and show them that they are important. You could make a difference in the life of a child. Just by spending time with the child you can set a positive example and expose him or her to God's Word. Even if there are restrictions about "religion" (unfortunately, it is commonplace in these times for organizations to try to squelch the teaching of the truth), you can set a positive example.

You can also give God the glory for the good things in your life. When God is as natural a part of your life as your mother or brother or best friend, you will naturally credit Him for everything you have and everything you are.

## 96. Offer to babysit for a couple so they can have an evening out

For new parents or parents of small children, time is precious – and "alone time" for the parents is almost nonexistent. Offer to babysit so that the parents can have a night out. You can give a new mom a break so that she can nap or go do something for herself. As parents, we give so much to our children, but it is important to take time for ourselves. You may need to remind parents of this, and be ready to step up, watch the kids and give the parents a much needed break.

## 97. Find a way to use your God given talents to bless others.

God has given each of us special talents and gifts. Are you good with a camera? Offer to take family photos for people who may not be able to afford them. Email the shots to them. You have just created a memory that they may not otherwise have.

Do you write? Pen an inspiration poem or story for someone. There are so many things that you can do, the possibilities are limitless! God gave you gifts, talents, so that you can use them for His glory. Use them to reach others and share God's Word with them.

## 98. Visit a retirement home

It is sad truth in our society that the elderly are often not valued as they should be. Many are dropped off in retirement homes and never receive visitors. It is a lonely, sad lift to feel forgotten by the outside world. Minister to these forgotten people by taking some time out of your life to visit with them.

Many homes have volunteer programs that allow people to come in and visit with the residents, play games and take them shopping. You have 168 hours a week. It will not hurt you to give an hour or two to someone else and make them feel loved and appreciated – make them feel special.

## 99. Sacrifice for others

Yes, it is good to give time, when you have some hours to spare or your money when you have a little extra, but what about then the giving takes something from you?

I believe that sometimes it is necessary to actually put yourself out to give to someone else. Give something up for yourself in order to give to someone else and you are truly giving.

## 100. Wash their feet

Washing a person's feet, in Jesus' time, was an ultimate act of servitude. Today, it is an expression used to describe true servitude to someone. When you give of yourself to someone, serve them in a humble, sincere manner, you are "washing their feet."

While nowadays few people's feet need washing, you can serve them in other ways. There are any number of ways that you can serve someone. If someone is ill, wash their hair for them. If someone's car breaks down, give them a ride to church. The key is to serve them with a humble manner and a glad heart.

## 101. Share the Good News of Salvation and Everlasting Life!

You can open the door with the 100 other simple ways to minister to others, but this, THIS, is what you do when you get that door open! Sometimes, of course that can't be done because God intends for you to be the seed planter in some cases. You are preparing the way for Him to bring someone else into that person's life to nurture what you have planted. Other times, though, you will have the wonderful opportunity to share with others how they can come to know Jesus and receive salvation.

John 3, Acts 2 and Acts 19:1-6 give a precise outline for salvation. You can start there. And you can change someone's life.

# 14

# CONCLUSION

As you have read this, you may have felt it was more a book of good deeds rather than a way of ministering to others. Yes, it is about doing good things, things to help people, life their spirits, so I guess that would be called "good deeds."

However, it is about taking it farther. It is about showing Jesus' face to people. Many times I have done these exact things, shown kindness to complete strangers, and it has opened conversations. Where you take it once the door is open is up to you.

Every morning when I pray, I ask God to use me. I ask Him to order my steps, to be my words, my thoughts, my actions as I go out into the world. I ask Him to kill off those parts of me that He finds offensive and fill me with Him so that I can be like Him. I ask that He put people in my path who need to hear His Word, need to know Him and that He will give me the words He wants them to hear – what they need to hear.

It is a very simple prayer, I know, but I pray it in earnest and God honors that. He has placed me in many situations where I have encountered people and God has moved and things have happened.

Once I was in a pharmacy and started talking to a woman. I did not know her, had never seen her before. She had come in because she had an injury that affected her mobility. I was in there because I had bronchitis. We both were picking up medication.

We talked for a bit and I felt God moving so I began to witness to her. She responded and the next thing I knew, she was sharing things with me about her past and her family – heartbreaking things. We talked for two hours. When we walked out of there, both she and I were completely healed! While we were talking, she just stopped and looked at me. "I don't feel any pain." She said. Then she moved around, sort of danced or jogged. We praised God for the healing. On my way home, though, I realized that I had not coughed once and my fever was gone. I did not take any of that medicine I had picked up even though the doctor had told me the day before (when he examined and diagnosed me) that I would be sick for a couple of weeks and cough for several weeks beyond that.

God is good!

Let the Spirit lead you, but when God prods you to move out of your comfort zone, be obedient. You will be blessed.

If I can do these things, approach strangers and help them or even strike up conversations with them, I *know* that you can do it. See, I am extremely shy. I have Asperger's and that makes me socially awkward. I am self conscious whenever I talk to people, even people I know, like at my church. There is always a nagging in the back of my mind that I will say something wrong, have an "Aspie moment." But I step beyond my comfort zone to reach out to these people. I can do it, so can you.

I also printed some cards with my name, email address (I am phone phobic and don't talk on one except to talk to my husband, kids, mother-in-law or my mother.) and my website, TheChristianAspie.com. Sometimes I give it to people I talk to. That may be an option for you as well, a way to break the ice, as they say.

We have been called to God's army and He wants us to reach out to as many people as we can. It is our job to populate the kingdom, whether we are the seed planters or the ones who do the watering.

So, what is God calling *you* to do? If you are reading this book, He has placed it in your hands via some means. I am guessing the answer, at least in part, is within these pages…

What are you going to do about it?

# ABOUT THE AUTHOR

Stephanie Mayberry is a Christian author whose passion for writing has become her ministry. An active member of the ministry team at The Life Church PWC in Manassas, VA, she has given her life to God and is realizing her calling of ministry through her writing.

As an adult with Asperger's Syndrome, she ministers to other Aspies (people with Asperger's Syndrome) through her blog, The Christian Aspie and several books she has written about being a Christian with Asperger's Syndrome. She also uses her experiences as a battered wife to reach out to people who have been through abuse and help them find healing through Jesus.

But God has also impressed upon her to write other titles as well. As she says, "God writes the words, I just hold the pen."

Stephanie lives in Virginia, just outside of Washington, D.C. with her infinitely patient husband and a dog genius.

# READ OTHER BOOKS
# BY STEPHANIE MAYBERRY AT

https://www.amazon.com/author/stephaniemayberry

http://www.smashwords.com/profile/view/StephanieMayberry

## VISIT STEPHANIE'S BLOG AT:

http://TheChristianAspie.com

## CONNECT WITH STEPHANIE

Email:  stephanie@thechristianaspie.com

Twitter:  http://twitter.com/fotojunkie

Facebook:
http://www.facebook.com/stephanie.a.mayberry

Made in the USA
Monee, IL
01 May 2021